Vegan Baking

Other cookery books by Linda Majzlik

Party Food for Vegetarians
Vegan Dinner Parties
Vegan Barbecues and Buffets
A Vegan Taste of Italy
A Vegan Taste of India
A Vegan Taste of Mexico
A Vegan Taste of the Caribbean
A Vegan Taste of the Middle East
A Vegan Taste of Eastern Europe
A Vegan Taste of Thailand
A Vegan Taste of France
A Vegan Taste of Greece
A Vegan Taste of North Africa
A Vegan Taste of Central America
A Vegan Taste of East Africa

VEGAN BAKING

Linda Majzlik

Our books may be ordered from any good bookshop

First published in 2001 by
Jon Carpenter Publishing
19 The Green, Charlbury, Oxfordshire OX7 3QA
☎ 01608 811378
Reprinted 2002, 2005, 2006, 2008, 2014
© Linda Majzlik 2001
Cover illustrations by Amanda Henriques © 2001

ISBN 978 1 897766 63 7

Printed in England by CPI Antony Rowe, Chippenham

CONTENTS

Small Cakes

Biscuits

Tray Bakes

No-Bake Cakes

Savoury Baking

INTRODUCTION

Although most supermarkets are becoming more enlightened these days and have started to stock a limited range of biscuits which contain no animal fats, it can still be quite difficult to find any shop-bought cakes made without eggs or other animal-derived ingredients. But with all the tempting aromas of home baking, who could resist a piece of home made cake or a freshly baked biscuit?

Home made vegan cakes, biscuits and tray bakes are no more difficult to make, are no less temptingly tasty and are lower in sugar and cholesterol than the traditional varieties. They can also make a valuable contribution to the vegan diet by providing protein, fibre, vitamins and minerals.

Whether you want to make a cake for a celebration, some little buns or biscuits for a teatime treat or some tray bake fingers to put in lunch boxes, you will find easy-to-make recipes for them here. Assuming that your baked goods don't 'disappear' immediately after baking—which is often the case!—this is how they should be stored. Once they are cold, the large cakes and loaves, small cakes and tray bakes should be wrapped in foil, stored in an airtight container in a cool cupboard and used within a week. (Some cakes need to be kept in the fridge, such as those containing fresh fruits—see individual recipes.) The no-bake cakes should be stored in an airtight container in the fridge and used within one week. The biscuits need to be stored in an airtight container in a cool cupboard and it is best to eat them within a couple of days of baking. All of the savouries are best eaten on the day of baking.

For longer storage, all the recipes can be successfully frozen. The large cakes and tray bakes can be frozen whole, or cut them into portions first so that you can just take out however many portions are needed. Either wrap the portions individually in foil or interleave them with greaseproof paper and wrap a few at a time in foil. Whichever way you use, don't forget to label and date the packages and use them within three months of freezing. To thaw allow at least 4 hours at room temperature for large cakes and loaves and 1–2 hours for individual portions, small cakes and biscuits, or leave them overnight in the fridge.

LARGE CAKES AND LOAVES

Marinated fruit cake

1lb/450g mixed cake fruit

9oz/250g fine wholemeal self raising flour

4oz/100g glacé cherries, washed, dried and quartered

4oz/100g vegan margarine

3oz/75g dark molasses sugar

2oz/50g dried dates, finely chopped

2oz/50g soya flour

4 fl.oz/125ml soya milk

juice and finely grated peel of 1 orange

juice and finely grated peel of 1 lemon

3 tablespoons brandy

1 rounded tablespoon molasses

1 rounded teaspoon ground allspice

1 rounded teaspoon ground mixed spice

extra brandy

Put the mixed fruit, glacé cherries, dates, orange and lemon juice and peel, 3 tablespoons of brandy, ground allspice and mixed spice in a bowl and stir well. Cover and leave overnight in a cool place or in the fridge.

Cream the margarine with the sugar and molasses in a large mixing bowl. Whisk the soya flour with the soya milk until creamy and add. Mix thoroughly, then stir in the marinated fruit mixture. Gradually add the flour until well combined.

Spoon the mixture into a lined and greased 8 inch/20cm diameter deep cake tin, press it down firmly and evenly and cover with foil. Bake in a preheated oven at 150°C/300°F/Gas mark 2 for 2 hours. Remove the foil and bake for a further 30–40 minutes, until a skewer comes out clean when inserted in the centre. Allow the cake to cool in the tin for 1 hour, then spoon about 2 table-spoonfuls of brandy over the top. Carefully remove the cake from the tin and put on a wire rack to cool completely before cutting.

Raspberry and hazelnut gateau

8oz/225g fine wholemeal self raising flour

2oz/50g hazelnuts, ground

2oz/50g demerara sugar

6 fl.oz/175ml sunflower oil

6 fl.oz/175ml soya milk

1 rounded tablespoon golden syrup

1 rounded teaspoon baking powder

$^1/_2$oz/15g hazelnuts, flaked

filling

6oz/175g raspberries

4oz/100g pot natural soya yoghurt

$^1/_2$oz/15g demerara sugar

1 fl.oz/25ml fresh apple juice

1 rounded teaspoon agar agar

First make the sponges. Put the ground hazelnuts, sugar, sunflower oil, soya milk and golden syrup in a mixing bowl and whisk thoroughly. Add the sifted flour and baking powder and mix well. Spoon the mixture into 2 lined and greased 7 inch/18cm diameter sandwich tins. Spread the mixture out evenly in the tins and sprinkle the flaked hazelnuts on top of one of the sponges, pressing these in lightly with the back of a spoon. Bake in a preheated oven at 180°C/350°F/Gas mark 4 for approximately 18 minutes until golden and springy. Allow to cool in the tins for 10 minutes, carefully transfer to a wire rack and leave to cool completely.

Mash the raspberries with the sugar and stir in the yoghurt. Dissolve the agar agar in the apple juice and heat gently until it begins to thicken. Add this to the raspberry mixture and stir well.

Cut each sponge in half horizontally to make 4 thin circles. Keep the sponge with the hazelnuts on top separate. Carefully put one of the sponges in a 7 inch/18cm diameter deep cake tin that has been lined with cling film. Spread a third of the filling evenly on top. Repeat these layers twice and finish with the hazelnut-topped sponge. Cover and chill for a few hours. Use the cling film to lift the gateau out of the tin, put it on a serving plate and cut it into wedges. The gateau can be stored in an airtight container in the fridge.

Mincemeat and almond cake

1lb/450g mincemeat

6oz/175g fine wholemeal self raising flour

2oz/50g ground almonds

2oz/50g vegan margarine

1oz/25g soya flour

4 tablespoons soya milk

2 tablespoons fresh apple juice

1 rounded tablespoon malt extract

flaked almonds

Cream the margarine with the malt extract in a large bowl. Mix the soya flour with the milk until smooth and add together with the ground almonds, mixing well. Stir in the mincemeat and apple juice and add the self raising flour. Mix thoroughly, then spoon the mixture evenly into a base-lined and greased 8 inch/20cm loaf tin. Press down firmly with the back of a spoon. Sprinkle some flaked almonds on top and press these in lightly. Cover with foil and bake in a preheated oven at 170°C/325°F/Gas mark 3 for 1¼ hours. Remove the foil and bake for a further 10 minutes until golden. Leave in the tin for 15 minutes, run a sharp knife around the edges and turn the cake out onto a wire rack to cool completely. Cut into slices to serve.

Blueberry and juniper loaf

1lb/450g plain wholemeal flour

3oz/75g dried blueberries

1oz/25g vegan margarine, melted

10 fl.oz/300ml soya milk

1 rounded tablespoon demerara sugar

1 rounded dessertspoon juniper berries

1 rounded teaspoon baking powder

Sift the flour and baking powder into a mixing bowl. Stir in the sugar and blueberries. Crush the juniper berries lightly with a pestle in a mortar, then blend them with the soya milk in a liquidiser. Pour the milk through a fine sieve into the bowl and discard the remains of the juniper berries. Add the melted margarine and mix thoroughly. Turn the dough out onto a floured board and knead well, then shape it into a 6 inch/15cm circle and put this on a greased baking sheet. Cut a cross shape on top with a sharp knife. Bake in a preheated oven at 180°C/350°F/Gas mark 4 for about 25 minutes, until the loaf is golden and sounds hollow when tapped on the underside. Allow to cool on a wire rack, cut into slices and spread with vegan margarine. This loaf is best eaten on the day of baking.

Chocolate, pear and pecan torte

9oz/250g fine wholemeal self raising flour

8oz/225g firm pear, peeled, cored and finely chopped

3oz/75g vegan chocolate bar, broken

1oz/25g demerara sugar

5 fl.oz/150ml soya milk

4 fl.oz/125ml sunflower oil

4 fl.oz/125ml fresh apple juice

1 teaspoon vanilla essence

1 rounded teaspoon baking powder

topping

1oz/25g cocoa powder

1oz/25g demerara sugar

1oz/25g vegan margarine

2 tablespoons water

2oz/50g pecans, finely chopped

Put the chocolate bar and soya milk in a bowl over a saucepan of boiling water. Stir until the chocolate melts and combines with the milk. Remove from the heat and pour into a mixing bowl. Add the sunflower oil, vanilla essence and pear and stir until well combined. Add the sifted flour and baking powder and then the juice and mix thoroughly. Spoon the mixture into a lined and greased 7 inch/18cm diameter cake tin, pressing it down firmly and evenly. Cover with foil and bake in a preheated oven at 180°C/350°F/Gas mark 4 for 20 minutes. Remove the foil and bake for a further 20 minutes until a skewer comes out clean when inserted in the centre. Allow to stand in the tin for 10 minutes, carefully transfer to a wire rack and leave to cool.

Mix the cocoa powder with the sugar and margarine until smooth. Add the water and stir until a spreading consistency is achieved. Spread half of this icing around the edge of the cake and roll in the chopped pecans until covered. Spread the rest of the icing on the top and sprinkle with the remaining chopped pecans. Press these in lightly with the back of a spoon before cutting the cake into portions. The torte can be stored in the fridge in an airtight container.

Sweet potato and peel cake

8oz/225g sweet potato, peeled and grated

8oz/225g cut mixed peel

8oz/225g fine wholemeal self raising flour

3oz/75g vegan margarine

2oz/50g flaked brown rice

1¹/₂oz/40g light muscovado sugar

4 fl.oz/125ml fresh orange juice

1 rounded tablespoon malt extract

1 tablespoon whisky

1 teaspoon aniseed

Put the sweet potato and orange juice in a small saucepan and bring to the boil. Simmer for 1 minute whilst stirring, then remove from the heat and allow to cool.

Cream the margarine with the sugar and malt extract. Stir in the sweet potato, mixed peel and aniseed. Add first the flaked brown rice, then the flour and whisky and mix thoroughly. Spoon the mixture into a lined and greased 7 inch/18cm diameter cake tin, level the top and cover loosely with foil. Bake in a preheated oven at 180°C/350°F/Gas mark 4 for 1 hour. Remove the foil and bake for 15 minutes more until golden brown. Leave the cake in the tin for 15 minutes, then carefully turn it out onto a wire rack and allow it to cool completely.

Strawberry and almond sponge

8oz/225g fine wholemeal self raising flour

6oz/175g strawberries, chopped

2oz/50g ground almonds

6 fl.oz/175ml sunflower oil

4oz/100g pot strawberry-flavoured soya yoghurt

2 rounded tablespoons sugar-free strawberry jam

extra sugar-free strawberry jam

2 fl.oz/50ml soya milk

2 rounded teaspoons baking powder

1/2oz/15g flaked almonds

Put the strawberries, sunflower oil, yoghurt, 2 rounded tablespoonfuls of jam and soya milk in a blender or liquidiser and blend until smooth. Pour into a large bowl and stir in the ground almonds. Add the sifted flour and baking powder and mix very well. Divide the mixture between 2 lined and greased 7 inch/18cm diameter sandwich tins, spreading it out evenly. Sprinkle the flaked almonds on top of one of the sponges and press them in lightly, then bake in a preheated oven at 180°C/350°F/Gas mark 4 for about 25 minutes until golden brown. Allow the sponges to cool in the tins for 5 minutes, then carefully turn them out onto a wire rack. When cool spread a thin layer of jam on the bottom sponge and place the almond-covered sponge on top. Store in an airtight container in the fridge.

Carob-covered rum, raisin and walnut savarin

6oz/175g fine wholemeal self raising flour

4oz/100g raisins, chopped

2oz/50g walnuts

2oz/50g vegan margarine, melted

1oz/25g demerara sugar

7 fl.oz/200ml soya milk, warmed

2 tablespoons rum

1 sachet easy-blend yeast

3oz/75g carob block, broken

Soak the raisins in the rum for 1 hour. Put the flour, sugar and yeast in a mixing bowl and stir well. Keep 8 walnut halves for decoration, finely chop the rest and add to the bowl together with the soaked raisins, melted margarine and soya milk. Mix thoroughly, then spoon the mixture evenly into a greased 7 inch/18cm ring mould. Cover and leave in a warm place for 1 hour until well risen. Uncover and bake in a preheated oven at 180°C/350°F/Gas mark 4 for 25 minutes. Run a sharp knife around the edge and carefully turn the ring out onto a baking sheet. Return to the oven for 5 minutes until golden, then transfer to a wire rack and allow to cool.

Melt the carob block in a bowl over a pan of boiling water. Spread the carob evenly all over the ring and arrange the 8 walnut halves on the top. Put in the fridge for a couple of hours until the carob has set before serving. The savarin can be stored in an airtight container in the fridge if required.

Upside-down peach and bran cake

4oz/100g bran sticks

4oz/100g fine wholemeal self raising flour

4oz/100g mixed cake fruit

2oz/50g vegan margarine

1oz/25g soft dark brown sugar

6 fl.oz/175ml fresh orange juice

5 fl.oz/150ml soya milk

1 rounded tablespoon malt extract

1 dessertspoon malt extract

1 teaspoon ground mixed spice

1 large firm peach, stoned and sliced

Soak the bran sticks in the orange juice for an hour. Put the margarine, sugar and tablespoonful of malt extract in a large saucepan and heat gently until melted, remove from the heat and add the soaked bran sticks, mixed cake fruit, soya milk, sifted flour and mixed spice. Mix thoroughly. Line and grease a 7 inch/18cm diameter cake tin. Warm the dessertspoonful of malt extract and pour into the tin. Arrange the peach slices in a circular pattern in the bottom and spoon the cake mixture evenly on top. Cover with foil and bake in a preheated oven at 180°C/350°F/Gas mark 4 for 30 minutes. Remove the foil and bake for a further 30–35 minutes until firm. Invert onto a wire rack and allow to cool before cutting. The cake can be kept in the fridge in an airtight container.

Orange, date and apricot loaf

8oz/225g fine wholemeal self raising flour

4oz/100g dried dates, finely chopped

2oz/50g dried apricots, finely chopped

2oz/50g vegan margarine

1oz/25g demerara sugar

juice and finely grated peel of 1 orange

4 fl.oz./125ml water

1 dessertspoon date syrup

1/2 teaspoon ground cinnamon

sesame seeds

Put the dates and water in a small saucepan and bring to the boil. Simmer for a few minutes until the liquid has been absorbed and the dates are soft, stirring frequently to prevent sticking. Remove from the heat and mash until smooth.

Cream the margarine, sugar and date syrup in a mixing bowl. Add the mashed dates, chopped apricots and orange peel and mix well. Pour the orange juice into a measuring jug and make up to 4 fl.oz/125ml if necessary with fresh fruit juice. Add half the sifted flour and cinnamon to the mixing bowl, together with half the juice. Mix, then add the remaining flour, cinnamon and juice. Mix thoroughly and spoon the mixture evenly into a base-lined and greased 8 inch/20cm loaf tin, pressing down firmly. Sprinkle the top with sesame seeds, cover with foil and bake in a preheated oven at 170°C/325°F/Gas mark 3 for 40 minutes. Remove the foil and bake for a further 15 minutes until golden. Leave the loaf to cool in the tin for 10 minutes, then run a sharp knife around the edges, turn it out onto a wire rack and allow it to cool completely. Cut into slices.

Coffee and pecan gateau

9oz/250g fine wholemeal self raising flour

2oz/50g pecans, grated

2oz/50g light muscovado sugar

7 fl.oz/200ml soya milk

6 fl.oz/175ml sunflower oil

1 rounded tablespoon golden syrup

1 tablespoon date syrup

1 tablespoon coffee powder or granules

filling

2oz/50g pecans, ground

2 tablespoons maple syrup

topping

4oz/100g carob bar, broken

1/2oz/15g pecans, grated

Put the sugar, soya milk, sunflower oil, golden syrup, date syrup and coffee powder or granules in a mixing bowl and whisk until smooth. Stir in the grated pecans, then the sifted flour. Divide the mixture between 2 lined and greased 7 inch/18cm diameter sandwich tins, spreading it evenly. Bake in a preheated oven at 180°C/350°F/Gas mark 4 for 18–20 minutes until golden and springy. Carefully put the sponges on a wire rack and allow to cool.

Mix the ground pecans with the maple syrup until smooth. Spread this filling on one of the sponges and place the other sponge on top.

Melt the carob bar in a bowl over a pan of boiling water. Cover the top and sides of the cake completely with the melted carob and sprinkle the grated pecans on the top, pressing them in lightly with the back of a spoon. Put the cake on a plate and refrigerate for a few hours until the carob has set. Store in an airtight container in the fridge.

Spiced carrot and nut loaf

8oz/225g carrots, scraped and chopped

6oz/175g fine wholemeal self raising flour

3oz/75g vegan margarine

2oz/50g mixed nuts, grated

2oz/50g sultanas, chopped

1¹/₂oz/40g light muscovado sugar

1oz/25g soya flour

1 rounded tablespoon golden syrup

4 tablespoons soya milk

1 rounded teaspoon ground coriander

¹/₂ teaspoon caraway seeds

¹/₂oz/15g mixed nuts, finely chopped

Steam the carrots until tender, then mash with a potato masher. Cream the margarine with the sugar and golden syrup in a large bowl, add the grated nuts, sultanas, mashed carrots and caraway seeds and stir well. Mix the soya flour with the soya milk until thick and creamy and add to the bowl together with the sifted flour and ground coriander. Mix thoroughly, then spoon the mixture into a base-lined and greased 8 inch/20cm loaf tin, pressing down firmly and evenly. Sprinkle the chopped nuts on top and press in lightly with the back of a spoon. Cover with foil and bake in a preheated oven at 180°C/350°F/Gas mark 4 for 1 hour. Remove the foil and bake the cake for a further 5 minutes until golden brown. Carefully turn out onto a wire rack to cool. Cut into slices to serve.

Nutty apple and date cake

9oz/250g eating apple, peeled, cored and finely chopped

8oz/225g fine wholemeal self raising flour

4oz/100g vegan margarine

4oz/100g dried dates, finely chopped

2oz/50g mixed nuts, ground

2oz/50g demerara sugar

1oz/25g soya flour

1 rounded tablespoon golden syrup

1 rounded tablespoon date syrup

4 tablespoons fresh apple juice

topping

1/2oz/15g mixed nuts, grated

1/2oz/15g fresh wholemeal breadcrumbs

1 rounded tablespoon demerara sugar

1/2 teaspoon ground allspice

Put the margarine, sugar, golden syrup and date syrup in a large saucepan and heat gently until melted. Remove from the heat and stir in the ground nuts, chopped dates and apple, and wholemeal flour. Whisk the soya flour with the apple juice and add. Stir thoroughly, then spoon the mixture into a lined and greased 7 inch/18cm cake tin. Press down firmly and evenly.

Mix the topping ingredients together, sprinkle on top of the cake and press in lightly with the back of a spoon. Cover with foil and bake in a preheated oven at 180°C/350°F/Gas mark 4 for 1 hour. Remove the foil and bake for a further 5 minutes until golden. Leave in the tin for 10 minutes, then transfer to a wire rack to cool completely.

Lemon, maple and hazelnut sandwich

8oz/225g fine wholemeal self raising flour

4oz/100g vegan margarine

3oz/75g muscovado sugar

1oz/25g hazelnuts, flaked

juice and finely grated peel of 1 lemon

2 tablespoons maple syrup

5 fl.oz/150ml soya milk

filling

2oz/50g hazelnuts, ground

2 tablespoons maple syrup

Cream the margarine with the sugar and maple syrup. Add the lemon juice and peel, sifted flour and soya milk and mix thoroughly. Divide the mixture between 2 lined and greased 7 inch/18cm diameter sandwich tins, spread out evenly and sprinkle the flaked hazelnuts on top of one of the sponges. Bake in a preheated oven at 180°C/350°F/Gas mark 4 for about 20 minutes until golden brown. Transfer the sponges to a wire rack and allow to cool.

Mix the ground hazelnuts with the maple syrup until well combined and spread this filling evenly over the plain sponge. Put the hazelnut-topped sponge on the filling and cut the sandwich into wedges.

Simnel cake

1½lb/675g marzipan

12oz/350g fine wholemeal self raising flour

5oz/150g vegan margarine

4oz/100g muscovado sugar

4oz/100g cut mixed peel

4oz/100g sultanas

4oz/100g raisins

4oz/100g currants

2oz/50g glacé cherries, washed, dried and chopped

1oz/25g soya flour

5 tablespoons soya milk

juice and finely grated peel of 1 orange

juice and finely grated peel of 1 lemon

1 rounded teaspoon ground mixed spice

sugar-free apricot jam

Put the mixed peel, sultanas, raisins, currants, glacé cherries, sugar, orange and lemon juice and peel and mixed spice in a large bowl and stir well. Cover and leave in a cool place or in the fridge overnight.

Rub the margarine into the flour, then gradually add to the fruit mixture. Whisk the soya flour with the soya milk until smooth and add. Mix thoroughly and spoon half of the mixture into a lined and greased 7 inch/18cm diameter cake tin. Take 4oz/100g of the marzipan and roll out to a 7inch/18cm circle. Place this over the cake mixture in the tin and press down firmly. Spoon the remaining cake mixture on top, again pressing down firmly and evenly. Cover with foil and bake in a preheated oven at 170°C/325°F/Gas mark 3 for 1 hour 40 minutes. Remove the foil and bake the cake for about 10 minutes more until golden brown. Allow to cool in the tin for 15 minutes, then transfer to a wire rack.

Spread the top and sides of the cake with a thin layer of apricot jam. Roll out 12oz/350g marzipan to cover the top and sides of the cake. Divide the remaining marzipan into 12 equal pieces and roll each piece into a small ball in the palm of the hand. Arrange the balls on top of the cake around the edge and place under a medium grill for a couple of minutes until lightly browned.

Breakfast loaf

6oz/175g bran buds

6oz/175g dried fruit salad, finely chopped

4oz/100g fine wholemeal self raising flour

2oz/50g wheatgerm

2oz/50g vegan margarine

6 fl.oz/175ml fresh orange juice

6 fl.oz/175ml strong black tea

2 rounded tablespoons sugar-free marmalade

2 tablespoons soya milk

linseed

Put the bran buds, orange juice and tea in a bowl and stir well. Cover and leave for 45 minutes.

Gently heat the margarine in a large saucepan until melted. Remove from the heat and stir in the marmalade, then add the soaked bran buds, chopped fruit, flour, wheatgerm and soya milk and mix thoroughly. Spoon the mixture into a base-lined and greased 8 inch/20cm loaf tin and press it down firmly and evenly with the back of a spoon. Sprinkle the top with linseed and press in lightly. Cover with foil and bake in a preheated oven at 180°C/350°F/Gas mark 4 for 40 minutes. Remove the foil and bake for 10–12 minutes more until golden. Leave in the tin for 10 minutes, then run a sharp knife around the edges and turn the loaf out onto a wire rack to cool completely. Cut into slices to serve.

Chocolate and walnut gateau

8oz/225g fine wholemeal self raising flour

2oz/50g walnuts, grated

1oz/25g light muscovado sugar

1/2oz/15g cocoa powder

7 fl.oz/200ml soya milk

5 fl.oz/150ml sunflower oil

1 rounded tablespoon golden syrup

1 tablespoon date syrup

filling

3oz/75g natural soya yoghurt

1 rounded tablespoon demerara sugar, ground

1 tablespoon cocoa powder

topping

4oz/100g vegan chocolate, broken

8 walnut halves

Put the sunflower oil, golden syrup, date syrup, muscovado sugar, grated walnuts and sifted cocoa powder in a mixing bowl and stir thoroughly. Add the sifted flour and the soya milk and mix until well combined. Divide the mixture between 2 lined and greased 7 inch/18cm diameter sandwich tins and spread it out evenly with the back of a spoon. Bake in a preheated oven at 170°C/325°F/Gas mark 3 for about 20 minutes until springy in the centres. Turn out onto a wire rack and allow to cool.

Mix the yoghurt with the demerara sugar and the cocoa powder until well combined and spread this filling evenly on one of the sponges. Place the other sponge on top.

Melt the chocolate bar in a bowl over a pan of boiling water. Cover the top and sides of the cake completely with the melted chocolate and arrange the walnut halves on top. Transfer the cake to a plate and refrigerate for a few hours until the chocolate has set. This gateau can be stored in an airtight container in the fridge.

Tropical fruit and nut cake

8oz/225g fine wholemeal self raising flour

4oz/100g dried mango

4oz/100g dried papaya

4oz/100g dried pineapple

4oz/100g vegan margarine

2oz/50g demerara sugar

2oz/50g brazil nuts, grated

1oz/25g desiccated coconut

1 rounded tablespoon golden syrup

1 tablespoon dark rum

1 rounded teaspoon ground allspice

3 fl.oz/75ml soya milk

6 fl.oz/175ml tropical fruit juice

Chop the dried fruits very finely and put them in a saucepan with the tropical fruit juice. Bring to the boil, cover and simmer gently for 10 minutes, stirring frequently. Remove from the heat.

Put the margarine, sugar and golden syrup in a large saucepan and heat gently until melted. Remove from the heat and stir in the fruit, brazil nuts, coconut and rum. Add the sifted flour and ground allspice and then the soya milk and mix thoroughly. Spoon the mixture into a base-lined and greased 8 inch/20cm loaf tin. Cover with foil and bake in a preheated oven at 180°C/350°F/Gas mark 4 for 45 minutes. Remove the foil and bake for about 10 minutes more until the cake is golden brown and a skewer comes out clean when inserted in the centre. Cool in the tin for 15 minutes, then run a sharp knife around the edges and turn out onto a wire rack to cool completely before cutting into slices.

Paradise cake

8oz/225g tin of pineapple in natural juice

8oz/225g fine wholemeal self raising flour

4oz/100g vegan margarine

4oz/100g dried dates, finely chopped

2oz/50g desiccated coconut

2oz/50g ground almonds

2oz/50g light muscovado sugar

1^{1}/$_{2}$oz/40g soya flour

4oz/100g banana, peeled and mashed

2 tablespoons maple syrup

^{1}/$_{2}$ teaspoon ground allspice

^{1}/$_{2}$oz/15g flaked almonds

Strain the pineapple juice into a small bowl, add the soya flour and whisk until smooth. Chop the pineapple finely and set aside.

Cream the margarine with the sugar and maple syrup in a mixing bowl. Add the banana, coconut and ground almonds and mix until smooth. Now add the soya flour mixture, chopped pineapple and dates and finally the sifted flour and ground allspice. Stir very well, then spoon the mixture into a lined and greased 7 inch/18cm diameter cake tin. Sprinkle the flaked almonds on top and press them in lightly with the back of a spoon. Cover with foil and bake in a preheated oven at 170°C/350°F/Gas mark 3 for 70 minutes. Remove the foil and bake for a further 10 minutes until golden. Leave in the tin for 15 minutes, then turn the cake out onto a wire rack to cool completely.

Malt loaf

8oz/225g fine wholemeal self raising flour

2oz/50g demerara sugar

2oz/50g bran

2oz/50g dried dates, finely chopped

2oz/50g sultanas

2oz/50g raisins

2oz/50g currants

10 fl.oz/300ml soya milk

2 rounded tablespoons malt extract

1 teaspoon ground mixed spice

$^1\!/_2$ teaspoon ground cinnamon

Mix the malt extract with the soya milk and sugar in a large bowl. Add the remaining ingredients and stir thoroughly. Spoon the mixture into a base-lined and greased 8 inch/20cm loaf tin and level the top. Cover loosely with foil and bake in a preheated oven at 180°C/350°F/Gas mark 4 for 40 minutes. Remove the foil and bake for 10 minutes more until the loaf is golden brown and a skewer comes out clean when inserted in the centre. Run a sharp knife around the edges, then turn out onto a wire rack and allow to cool. Cut into slices and spread with vegan margarine or sugar-free jam.

Spiced fruit cake

12oz/350g fine wholemeal self raising flour

4oz/100g dried apricots, finely chopped

4oz/100g dried dates, finely chopped

4oz/100g sultanas

4oz/100g raisins

3oz/75g molasses sugar

1oz/25g soya flour

1 banana (approx. 6oz/175g), peeled and mashed

6 fl.oz/175ml sunflower oil

6 fl.oz/175ml fresh fruit juice

1 rounded tablespoon molasses

1 teaspoon ground mixed spice

1 teaspoon ground allspice

Put the sunflower oil, fruit juice, molasses and sugar in a mixing bowl and stir until well combined. Add the apricots, dates, sultanas, raisins and banana and leave for 30 minutes.

Sift the wholemeal flour with the soya flour, mixed spice and allspice into the bowl. Mix thoroughly until a stiff consistency is obtained. Spoon the mixture into a lined and greased 7 inch/18cm diameter cake tin, level the top with the back of a dampened spoon and make an indent in the centre. Cover with foil and bake in a preheated oven at 170°C/325°F/Gas mark 3 for 1 hour 15 minutes. Remove the foil and bake for another 15 minutes until golden and a skewer comes out clean when inserted in the centre. Leave to cool in the tin for 15 minutes, then turn out onto a wire rack.

Banana, pecan and date loaf

1lb/450g ripe bananas, peeled and mashed

2oz/50g pecans, grated

2oz/50g dried dates, finely chopped

8oz/225g fine wholemeal self raising flour

4 fl.oz/125ml sunflower oil

1 rounded tablespoon golden syrup

sesame seeds

Mix the sunflower oil with the golden syrup, bananas, pecans and dates. Stir in the flour and mix thoroughly. Spoon the mixture into a base-lined and greased 8 inch/20cm loaf tin, level the top and sprinkle with sesame seeds. Cover loosely with foil and bake in a preheated oven at 180°C/350°F/Gas mark 4 for 40 minutes. Remove the foil, then bake for a further 20 minutes until a skewer comes out clean when inserted in the centre and the loaf is golden brown. Run a sharp knife round the edges of the tin, turn the loaf out onto a wire rack and allow it to cool. Cut into slices to serve.

Cherry, coconut and nut cake

8oz/225g silken tofu, mashed

8oz/225g fine wholemeal self raising flour

8oz/225g glacé cherries, washed and dried

4oz/100g mixed nuts, grated

4oz/100g mixed cake fruit

4oz/100g vegan margarine

3oz/75g demerara sugar

2oz/50g desiccated coconut

1oz/25g soya flour

3 fl.oz/75ml soya milk

1/2 teaspoon ground allspice

Cream the margarine with the sugar in a mixing bowl. Add the tofu and mix well. Chop 6oz/175g of the glacé cherries and add to the bowl together with the grated nuts, coconut, mixed cake fruit and soya flour. Mix, stir in the soya milk and add the sifted flour and allspice. Combine thoroughly, then spoon the mixture into a base-lined and greased 9 inch/23cm loaf tin, pressing it down firmly and evenly. Cut the remaining cherries in half and push these lightly into the top of the cake. Cover with foil and bake in a preheated oven at 170°C/325°F/Gas mark 3 for 1 hour. Remove the foil and bake for 10–15 minutes more until browned. Leave the cake in the tin for 15 minutes, run a sharp knife round the edges and carefully remove it from the tin. Allow to cool on a wire rack.

SMALL CAKES

Pistachio and date buns

Makes 8

6oz/175g fine wholemeal self raising flour

2oz/50g shelled pistachios, ground

2oz/50g vegan margarine

1oz/25g muscovado sugar

1/2oz/15g soya flour

3 fl.oz/75ml soya milk

filling

2oz/50g dried dates, finely chopped

2 fl.oz/50ml water

Rub the margarine into the flour and stir in the pistachios and sugar. Mix the soya flour with the milk until creamy and add. Combine thoroughly until a soft dough forms. Turn out onto a floured board and roll into a sausage shape. Cut into 8 equal portions and roll each one into a ball in the palm of the hand. Put on a greased baking sheet and press a thumb into the top of each ball to make a cavity. Bake in a preheated oven at 180°C/350°F/Gas mark 4 for 10 minutes, then remove from the oven and press a thumb into the holes again. Return to the oven for about 8 minutes until golden. Transfer to a wire rack and allow to cool.

Put the dates and water in a small saucepan and bring to the boil. Simmer until the dates soften and the mixture thickens. Remove from the heat and mash. Allow to cool, then spoon a little of the date mixture into the hollow in each bun.

Orchard fruit buns

Makes 9

4oz/100g fine wholemeal self raising flour

2oz/50g dried apple, finely chopped

2oz/50g dried pear, finely chopped

2oz/50g vegan margarine

2oz/50g sugar-free pear and apple spread

1/2oz/15g soya flour

4 fl.oz/125ml fresh apple juice

1/4 teaspoon ground cloves

Cream the margarine with the pear and apple spread. Whisk the soya flour with the apple juice until smooth and add to the bowl together with the dried apple and pear. Stir well, then add the sifted flour and ground cloves. Mix thoroughly and divide the mixture between 9 paper cake cases that have been put into the holes of a muffin tin. Bake the buns in a preheated oven at 170°C/325°F/Gas mark 3 for 20–25 minutes until golden. Leave in the tin for 5 minutes, then transfer to a wire rack to cool completely.

Mincemeat and almonds tarts   *Makes 12*

pastry

4oz/100g fine wholemeal self raising flour

1¹/₂oz/40g vegan margarine

water

filling

6oz/175g mincemeat

topping

3oz/75g fine wholemeal self raising flour

1oz/25g ground almonds

1oz/25g vegan margarine

1oz/25g light muscovado sugar

¹/₂oz/15g soya flour

6 fl.oz/175ml soya milk

¹/₂ teaspoon almond essence

flaked almonds

Rub the margarine for the pastry into the flour and add enough water to bind. Turn out onto a floured board and roll out thinly. Cut into 12 2¹/₂ inch/6cm diameter circles using a biscuit cutter, gathering up the dough and re-rolling until it is used up. Place the circles in a 12-holed greased muffin tin. Divide the mincemeat between the pastry circles.

To make the topping cream the margarine with the sugar. Mix the ground almonds, soya flour and almond essence with the soya milk until smooth and add, together with the flour. Stir well. Spoon the topping over the mincemeat, covering it completely, and sprinkle with flaked almonds. Bake in a preheated oven at 180°C/350°F/Gas mark 4 for approximately 25 minutes until golden. Run a sharp knife around the edges and carefully transfer the tarts to a wire rack. Serve either warm or cold.

Saffron and poppy seed buns   *Makes 12*

8oz/225g fine wholemeal self raising flour

2oz/50g vegan margarine, melted

2oz/50g sultanas

1oz/25g demerara sugar

$^1/_2$oz/15g poppy seeds

1 sachet easy-blend yeast

7 fl.oz/200ml soya milk

$^1/_2$ teaspoon saffron strands

6 glacé cherries, halved

Put the flour, sultanas, sugar, poppy seeds and yeast in a mixing bowl and stir well. Add the saffron strands to the soya milk and heat gently until warm. Pour the saffron milk and the melted margarine over the dry ingredients and mix thoroughly. Place paper cake cases in a 12-holed muffin tin, divide the mixture between them and leave in a warm place for 1 hour until well risen. Put half a glacé cherry on top of each bun and bake them in a preheated oven at 180°C/350°F/Gas mark 4 for about 20 minutes until golden brown. Transfer the buns to a wire rack to cool.

Plain scones   *Makes 8*

8oz/225g fine wholemeal self raising flour

2oz/50g vegan margarine

2 rounded teaspoons baking powder

approx. 4 fl.oz/125ml soya milk

extra soya milk

Sift the flour and baking powder into a mixing bowl. Rub in the margarine, then gradually add the soya milk until a soft dough forms. Turn out onto a floured board and roll out to about $^3/_4$ inch/2cm thick. Cut into $2^1/_2$ inch/6cm rounds with a biscuit cutter, gathering up the dough and re-rolling until it is all used up. Put the scones on a greased baking sheet and brush the tops with soya milk. Bake in a preheated oven at 180°C/350°F/Gas mark 4 for 12–15 minutes until golden. Transfer to a wire rack to cool. Slice in half and spread with vegan margarine or sugar-free jam.

For the recipes below, proceed as for plain scones and add the extra ingredients before stirring in the soya milk.

Prune and walnut scones

4oz/100g prunes, stoned and finely chopped
1oz/25g walnuts, finely chopped

Mixed fruit and spice scones

2 rounded teaspoons ground mixed spice
2oz/50g currants
2oz/50g cut mixed peel
2oz/50g sultanas

Date and pecan scones

4oz/100g dried dates, finely chopped
1oz/25g pecans, chopped

Muffins

Makes 9

basic mixture
6oz/175g fine wholemeal self raising flour

1¹/₂oz/40g demerara sugar

2oz/50g vegan margarine

4 fl.oz/125ml soya milk

¹/₂oz/15g soya flour

3 tablespoons water

Mix the self raising flour with the sugar in a large bowl. Whisk the soya flour with the water until thick and smooth and add, together with the melted margarine and the soya milk. Divide the mixture between 9 paper cake cases that have been put in the holes of a muffin tin. Bake in a preheated oven at 180°C/350°F/Gas mark 4 for about 25 minutes until golden. Leave to cool on a wire rack.

Banana, apricot and walnut muffins

1 ripe banana, peeled and mashed

2oz/50g dried no-soak apricots, finely chopped

1oz/25g walnuts, finely chopped

Add to the basic mixture.

Mixed fruit and spice muffins

1oz/25g sultanas

1oz/25g raisins

1oz/25g dried dates, finely chopped

1oz/25g cut mixed peel

1 rounded teaspoon ground mixed spice

Add to the basic mixture and top each muffin with half a glacé cherry before baking.

Chocolate chip and raisin muffins

> 1 rounded tablespoon cocoa powder
>
> 1^1/$_2$oz/40g vegan chocolate, cut into small chips
>
> 1^1/$_2$oz/40g raisins

Add to the basic mixture.

Carob, hazelnut and carrot muffins

> 2oz/50g carrot, scraped and grated
>
> ^{1}/$_2$oz/15g hazelnuts, flaked
>
> 1 rounded tablespoon carob and hazelnut spread

Melt the carob and hazelnut spread with the margarine and add to the basic mixture with the carrot and flaked hazelnuts.

Apple, raisin and clove muffins

> 8oz/225g cooking apple, peeled, cored and grated
>
> 2oz/50g raisins
>
> 1 rounded tablespoon golden syrup
>
> ^{1}/$_2$ teaspoon ground cloves

Omit the water in the basic recipe and use only 3 fl.oz/75ml soya milk. Whisk the soya flour with the soya milk and melt the golden syrup with the margarine. Mix all ingredients well.

Mincemeat muffins

> 6oz/175g mincemeat

Add to the basic mixture.

Coconut and cherry muffins

> 1oz/25g desiccated coconut
>
> 3oz/75g glacé cherries

Use 5oz/150g wholemeal self raising flour only. Keep 9 glacé cherry halves to put on top of the muffins. Chop the remaining cherries and add to the mixture together with the coconut.

Date and ginger muffins

> 3oz/75g dried dates, finely chopped
>
> 1oz/25g stem ginger, finely chopped
>
> $1/2$ teaspoon ground ginger

Add to the basic mixture.

Coconut rockies   *Makes 12*

> 6oz/175g desiccated coconut
>
> 2oz/50g vegan margarine
>
> 1oz/25g demerara sugar
>
> 1oz/25g cornflour
>
> 1oz/25g soya flour
>
> 10 fl.oz/300ml water

Gently heat the margarine in a large saucepan until melted. Remove from the heat and stir in the cornflour and soya flour, mixing thoroughly, then add the water. Bring to the boil whilst stirring and continue stirring until the mixture becomes thick. Take off the heat and add the coconut and sugar. Mix very well, then spoon the mixture onto a greased baking sheet in 12 heaps. Bake in a preheated oven at 180°C/350°F/Gas mark 4 for 30–35 minutes until golden brown. Transfer to a wire rack and allow to cool.

Marbled buns   *Makes 10*

6oz/175g fine wholemeal self raising flour

1oz/25g demerara sugar

1oz/25g soya flour

5 fl.oz/150ml sunflower oil

5 fl.oz/150ml soya milk

1 rounded tablespoon golden syrup

1oz/25g wheatgerm

1 banana, approx. 6oz/175g, peeled and mashed

$^{1}/_{2}$oz/15g cocoa powder

3 tablespoons soya milk

Put the golden syrup, sugar, sunflower oil and soya flour in a large saucepan and heat gently whilst stirring until well combined. Remove from the heat and add the flour and 5 fl.oz/150ml soya milk. Mix thoroughly. Put half the mixture in another bowl. Add the mashed banana and wheatgerm to one half of the mixture and the cocoa powder and 3 tablespoonfuls of soya milk to the other.

Line 10 holes of a muffin tin with paper cake cases. Spoon alternate teaspoon-fuls of the two mixtures into the cases until used up. Bake in a preheated oven at 180°C/350°F/Gas mark 4 for 18–20 minutes until golden. Leave on a wire rack to cool.

Nutty rock cakes

Makes 12

8oz/225g fine wholemeal self raising flour

4oz/100g vegan margarine

4oz/100g mixed cake fruit

2oz/50g mixed nuts, chopped

2oz/50g light muscovado sugar

1oz/25g soya flour

2 rounded tablespoons malt extract

6 tablespoons water

Rub the margarine into the flour and stir in the mixed cake fruit, nuts and sugar. Put the malt extract and water in a small saucepan and heat gently until they combine. Remove from the heat and whisk in the soya flour until smooth, then add to the other ingredients and mix thoroughly. Spoon the mixture in 12 mounds on a greased baking sheet. Bake in a preheated oven at 170°C/325°F/Gas mark 3 for 12–15 minutes until golden brown. Carefully put onto a wire rack.

Chocolate chip and cherry buns   *Makes 12*

8oz/225g fine wholemeal self raising flour

4oz/100g vegan margarine

2oz/50g light soft brown sugar

4oz/100g glacé cherries, washed and dried

2oz/50g vegan chocolate, cut into chips

4oz/100g pot black cherry-flavoured soya yoghurt

1/2oz/15g soya flour

3 fl.oz/75ml soya milk

Rub the margarine into the flour and stir in the sugar. Keep 6 glacé cherries for decoration and chop the rest. Add to the bowl together with the chocolate chips and yoghurt. Whisk the soya flour with the soya milk and mix thoroughly with the other ingredients. Spoon the mixture into 12 paper cake cases in a muffin tin. Cut the reserved glacé cherries in half and put one half on top of each cake. Bake in a preheated oven at 180°C/350°F/Gas mark 4 for about 25 minutes until golden. Transfer to a wire rack.

Chestnut and cranberry rock buns   *Makes 12*

6oz/175g fine wholemeal self raising flour

4oz/100g shelled chestnuts, grated

3oz/75g cranberry sauce

3oz/75g dried cranberries, chopped

2oz/50g vegan margarine

5 fl.oz/150ml soya milk

Put the chestnut and the soya milk in a saucepan and bring to the boil. Simmer for 3 minutes, stirring frequently to prevent sticking. Remove from the heat and allow to cool. Cream the margarine with the cranberry sauce. Stir in the chestnut mixture and the chopped cranberries, then add the flour and mix thoroughly. Divide the mixture between the 12 holes of a greased bun tin. Bake in a preheated oven at 180°C/350°F/Gas mark 4 for about 25 minutes until golden brown. Carefully transfer the buns to a wire rack and allow to cool.

Marmalade and malt cakes   *Makes 9*

5oz/150g fine wholemeal self raising flour

4oz/100g sultanas

2oz/50g vegan margarine

1oz/25g soya flour

2 rounded tablespoons chunky marmalade

1 rounded tablespoon malt extract

2 tablespoons fresh orange juice

1/4 teaspoon ground mace

Heat the margarine, marmalade and malt extract in a large saucepan until melted and well combined. Remove from the heat, add the remaining ingredients and mix thoroughly. Divide the mixture between 9 paper cake cases. Bake in a preheated oven at 170°C/325°F/Gas mark 3 for about 20 minutes until browned. Put on a wire rack to cool.

BISCUITS

Almond and maizemeal shortbread

Makes 8

4oz/100g ground almonds

4oz/100g maizemeal

2oz/50g demerara sugar

2oz/50g vegan margarine

3 tablespoons soya milk

$^{1}/_{2}$ teaspoon almond essence

Mix the ground almonds with the maizemeal, rub in the margarine and stir in the sugar. Add the almond essence and soya milk and mix thoroughly. Spoon the mixture into a lined and greased 7 inch/18cm diameter flan tin and press it down firmly and evenly with the back of a spoon. Cut through into 8 equal triangles. Bake in a preheated oven at 180°C/350°F/Gas mark 4 for 15–18 minutes until golden. Cut into the 8 triangles again and carefully transfer them to a wire rack.

Orange, alfalfa and cardamom cookies

Makes approx 14

5oz/150g fine oatmeal

2oz/50g fine wholemeal self raising flour

1oz/25g alfalfa seeds, ground

2 fl.oz/50ml sunflower oil

juice and finely grated peel of 1 orange

1 rounded tablespoon golden syrup

9 cardamom pods

extra alfalfa seeds

Remove the husks from the cardamom pods and grind the seeds using a pestle and mortar. Pour the orange juice into a measuring jug and make up to 3 fl.oz/75ml with fresh orange juice if necessary. Put the juice in a mixing bowl with the orange peel, golden syrup, sunflower oil and ground alfalfa seeds. Stir until well combined, then add the ground cardamom seeds, the oatmeal and the flour and mix thoroughly. Place rounded dessertspoonfuls of the mixture on a greased baking sheet, leaving sufficient room to flatten each mound. Neaten the cookies, using a damp fork. Sprinkle with alfalfa seeds and bake in a preheated oven at 170°C/325°F/Gas mark 3 for about 15 minutes until golden brown. Put on a wire rack to cool.

Cherry and macadamia oat cakes   *Makes approx 25*

4oz/100g glacé cherries, washed, dried and finely chopped

2oz/50g macadamia nuts, grated

2oz/50g porridge oats

2oz/50g medium oatmeal

2oz/50g vegan margarine

1oz/25g light muscovado sugar

1oz/25g soya flour

1 tablespoon soya milk

Cream the margarine with the sugar, then work in the cherries, nuts, porridge oats, oatmeal and soya flour. Add the soya milk and mix thoroughly until a soft dough forms. Gather into a ball and roll out the quite sticky dough on a well floured board to approximately ¼ inch/5mm thick. Cut out 2¼ inch/5.5cm rounds with a biscuit cutter, gathering up the dough and re-rolling until it is all used up. Place the rounds on a greased baking sheet and bake in a preheated oven at 180°C/350°F/Gas mark 4 for 8–10 minutes until just golden. Allow to cool for 10 minutes and then carefully transfer to a wire rack to cool completely.

Walnut and oatmeal crunchies *Makes approx 24*

4oz/100g medium oatmeal

2oz/50g walnuts, grated

2oz/50g cornflour

2oz/50g vegan margarine

1¹/₂oz/40g demerara sugar

1 tablespoon date syrup

Cream the margarine with the sugar and date syrup. Stir in the walnuts, then work in the oatmeal and cornflour until the mixture binds together. Turn out onto a floured board and roll out to approximately ¹/₄ inch/5mm thick. Cut into 2¹/₄ inch/5.5cm circles with a biscuit cutter and carefully transfer them to a greased baking sheet using a palette knife. Gather up the dough and re-roll until it is all used. Bake in a preheated oven at 180°C/350°F/Gas mark 4 for 8–10 minutes until golden brown and leave to cool on a wire rack.

Spiced cherry and oat cookies *Makes 12*

4oz/100g porridge oats

2oz/50g fine wholemeal self raising flour

2oz/50g glacé cherries, washed, dried and finely chopped

2oz/50g vegan margarine

1¹/₂oz/40g demerara sugar

2 tablespoons soya milk

¹/₂ teaspoon ground allspice

Cream the margarine with the sugar and add the porridge oats, cherries, sifted flour and ground allspice. Mix in the milk until the mixture binds together. Take rounded dessertspoonfuls of the dough and roll into balls in the palm of the hand. Flatten each ball into a biscuit shape and put them on a greased baking sheet. Bake in a preheated oven at 180°C/350°F/Gas mark 4 for about 12 minutes until browned and carefully transfer to a wire rack to cool.

Nutty muesli and oatmeal bites   *Makes approx 12*

4oz/100g muesli

4oz/100g medium oatmeal

2oz/50g fine wholemeal self raising flour

2oz/50g vegan margarine

1oz/25g light soft brown sugar

1 rounded tablespoon mixed nut butter

4 tablespoons fresh fruit juice

Put the margarine, nut butter and sugar in a large saucepan and heat gently until melted. Remove from the heat. Finely chop any large nuts or pieces of fruit in the muesli, then add the muesli, oatmeal and flour to the pan. Stir well, add the fruit juice and mix thoroughly. Take rounded dessertspoonfuls of the mixture and roll into balls in the palm of the hand. Flatten each ball into a biscuit shape and put on a greased baking sheet. Bake in a preheated oven at 180°C/350°F/Gas mark 4 for about 15 minutes until golden. Leave to cool on a wire rack.

Cashew nut and oatbran fingers   *Makes 10*

4oz/100g fine wholemeal self raising flour

2oz/50g cashew nuts, grated

2oz/50g oatbran

2oz/50g vegan margarine

1 rounded tablespoon cashew nut butter

1 rounded tablespoon golden syrup

2 tablespoons oatmilk or soya milk

Gently heat the margarine, cashew nut butter and golden syrup in a large saucepan until melted. Remove from the heat and stir in the cashews, oatbran and flour. Add the milk and mix thoroughly. Spoon the mixture into a lined and greased 7 inch/18cm square flan tin and press it down firmly and evenly with the back of a spoon. Cut the dough in half with a sharp knife, then into 10 equal-sized fingers. Bake in a preheated oven at 180°C/350°F/Gas mark 4 for 12–15 minutes until golden brown. Score through into the 10 fingers again and transfer them to a wire rack to cool.

Almond and currant cookies   *Makes approx 15*

> 4oz/100g fine wholemeal self raising flour
>
> 2oz/50g ground almonds
>
> 2oz/50g currants
>
> 2oz/50g vegan margarine
>
> 1oz/25g light muscovado sugar
>
> 1 rounded tablespoon almond butter
>
> 2 tablespoons soya milk
>
> $^1/_2$ teaspoon almond essence

Rub the margarine into the flour and stir in the ground almonds, currants and sugar. Combine the almond butter with the soya milk and almond essence until smooth. Add to the mixture and stir thoroughly until it binds together. Take rounded dessertspoonfuls of the dough and roll into balls in the palm of the hand. Flatten each ball into a biscuit shape and put them on a greased baking sheet. Bake in a preheated oven at 180°C/350°F/Gas mark 4 for about 10 minutes until browned. Carefully put the cookies on a wire rack.

Pear and ginger oaties   *Makes approx 14*

> 2oz/50g dried pears, finely chopped
>
> 2oz/50g plain wholemeal flour
>
> 2oz/50g porridge oats
>
> 2oz/50g medium oatmeal
>
> 2oz/50g vegan margarine

1oz/25g demerara sugar

2 fl.oz/50ml fresh apple juice

1 rounded teaspoon ground ginger

Put the pears and apple juice in a small saucepan and bring to the boil. Cook gently for a few minutes whilst stirring until the juice has been absorbed and the pears are soft. Remove from the heat and mash until smooth.

Cream the margarine with the sugar and add the mashed pears. Mix until well combined, then work in the sifted flour, ground ginger, porridge oats and oatmeal. Gather the mixture together and turn out onto a floured board. Roll out to approximately $^1/_4$ inch/5mm thick and cut into $2^1/_2$ inch/6cm rounds with a biscuit cutter. Gather up the dough and re-roll until it is used up. Transfer the rounds carefully to a greased baking sheet and bake in a preheated oven at 170°C/325°F/Gas mark 3 for 12–15 minutes until just golden. Leave on the baking sheet for 5 minutes before transferring the oaties to a wire rack to cool completely.

Fruity almond cookies   *Makes approx 20*

6oz/175g fine wholemeal self raising flour

2oz/50g vegan margarine

1oz/25g glacé cherries, washed, dried and finely chopped

1oz/25g cut mixed peel

1oz/25g currants

1oz/25g sultanas, chopped

1oz/25g flaked almonds, finely chopped

5 tablespoons soya milk

1 rounded tablespoon golden syrup

$^1/_2$ teaspoon almond essence

Put the margarine, almond essence and golden syrup in a large saucepan and heat gently until melted. Remove from the heat. Mix the fruit and almonds with the flour and add to the saucepan, together with the soya milk. Mix thoroughly until the mixture binds. Take heaped teaspoonfuls and place on a greased baking sheet. Flatten and shape each heap into a biscuit with damp fingers. Bake in a preheated oven at 180°C/350°F/Gas mark 4 for about 12 minutes until golden brown. Transfer to a wire rack and allow to cool.

Peanut and raisin cookies
Makes 12

> 6oz/175g fine wholemeal self raising flour
>
> 2oz/50g shelled and husked peanuts, finely chopped
>
> 2oz/50g raisins, finely chopped
>
> 2oz/50g vegan margarine
>
> 1oz/25g demerara sugar
>
> 1 rounded tablespoon peanut butter
>
> 3 tablespoons soya milk

Gently heat the margarine, sugar and peanut butter in a large saucepan until melted. Remove from the heat and stir in the peanuts and raisins. Add first the sifted flour and then the soya milk and mix thoroughly. Roll heaped dessert-spoonfuls of the mixture into balls in the palm of the hand, flatten each ball and place these rounds on a greased baking sheet. Bake in a preheated oven at 180°C/350°F/Gas mark 4 for 10–12 minutes until brown. Leave to cool on a wire rack.

Pine kernel and poppy seed crunchies
Makes approx 16

> 2oz/50g pine kernels, toasted and grated
>
> 2oz/50g fine wholemeal self raising flour
>
> 1oz/25g poppy seeds
>
> 1oz/25g vegan margarine
>
> 1oz/25g demerara sugar

1oz/25g soya flour

3 tablespoons soya milk

Cream the margarine with the sugar and work in the pine kernels, poppy seeds, soya flour and wholemeal flour until the mixture resembles fine bread-crumbs. Add the soya milk and mix until everything binds together. Turn the dough out onto a floured board and roll out to about ¼ inch/5mm thick. Cut into 2 inch/5cm squares with a fluted biscuit cutter and transfer these to a greased baking sheet. Gather up the dough and re-roll until it has been used up. Bake in a preheated oven at 180°C/350°F/Gas mark 4 for about 15 minutes until golden. Leave the crunchies on the baking sheet for 5 minutes before putting them on a wire rack to cool completely.

Spiced coconut and oatbran stars   *Makes approx 25*

4oz/100g fine wholemeal self raising flour

2oz/50g desiccated coconut

2oz/50g oatbran

2oz/50g vegan margarine

1oz/25g demerara sugar

1 rounded tablespoon golden syrup

2 tablespoons soya milk

1 teaspoon ground allspice

Put the margarine, golden syrup and sugar in a saucepan and heat gently until melted. Remove from the heat and stir in the sifted flour and allspice, the coconut and the oatbran. Add the soya milk and mix thoroughly until a soft dough forms. Turn out onto a floured board and roll out to approximately ¼ inch/5mm thick. Cut into stars with a 2½ inch/6cm star-shaped biscuit cutter and put them on a greased baking sheet. Gather up the dough and re-roll until it is all used. Bake in a preheated oven at 180°C/350°F/Gas mark 4 for about 8 minutes until just golden. Leave for 5 minutes and then carefully put the stars on a wire rack.

Lemon shorties

Makes approx 25

4oz/100g wholewheat semolina

2oz/50g cornflour

2oz/50g fine wholemeal self raising flour

2oz/50g vegan margarine

1oz/25g light muscovado sugar

1 rounded tablespoon golden syrup

juice and finely grated peel of 1 small lemon

Cream the margarine with the sugar and the golden syrup. Add the remaining ingredients and mix thoroughly until a soft dough is formed. Turn out onto a floured board and roll out to about $^1/_4$ inch/5mm thick. Cut into rounds using a $2^1/_4$ inch/5.5cm biscuit cutter, gathering up the dough and re-rolling until it is used up. Place the rounds on a greased baking sheet and bake in a preheated oven at 180°C/350°F/Gas mark 4 for approximately 10 minutes until just golden. Transfer to a wire rack and allow to cool.

Fig and cinnamon sandwich biscuits

Makes 20

8oz/225g fine wholemeal self raising flour

3oz/75g vegan margarine

1oz/25g light soft brown sugar

1 rounded teaspoon ground cinnamon

approx. 5 tablespoons soya milk

filling

8oz/225g dried, ready-to-eat figs, finely chopped

6 fl.oz/175ml fresh orange juice

Put the figs and orange juice in a saucepan and bring to the boil. Simmer gently until the juice has been absorbed and the mixture thickens, stirring frequently to prevent sticking. Remove from the heat and mash with a potato masher. Allow to cool.

Sift the flour with the cinnamon into a mixing bowl. Rub in the margarine, then stir in the sugar. Gradually add the milk until a soft dough forms. Divide the dough into 2 equal pieces and roll each one out into an oblong shape measuring 10 x 8 inches/25 x 20cm. Neaten the edges and spread the fig mixture evenly over one of the pieces of dough. Put the other piece on top and press down lightly. Cut the sandwich into 20 2 inch/5cm squares and carefully transfer these to a greased baking sheet, neatening the edges as you go. Make a couple of slits in the top of each square and bake them in a preheated oven at 180°C/350°F/Gas mark 4 for 12–15 minutes until golden brown. Leave to cool on a wire rack.

Brazil nut and oat fingers   *Makes 12*

6oz/175g medium oatmeal

2oz/50g oatbran

2oz/50g brazil nuts, grated

2oz/50g fine wholemeal self raising flour

2oz/50g vegan margarine

1oz/25g light soft brown sugar

2 tablespoons date syrup

2 tablespoons soya milk

Cream the margarine with the sugar and date syrup. Work in the dry ingredients, then add the soya milk and mix thoroughly. Line a 7 inch/18cm square baking tin with clingfilm, leaving an overhang. Spoon the mixture into the tin and press down firmly and evenly. Cut into 12 equal-sized bars. Use the clingfilm to lift the fingers out of the tin and carefully put them on a greased baking sheet. Bake in a preheated oven at 180°C/350°F/Gas mark 4 for about 15 minutes until golden. Cool on a wire rack.

Carob chip and coffee buttons

Makes 12

4oz/100g fine wholemeal self raising flour

2oz/50g vegan margarine

1oz/25g light muscovado sugar

1oz/25g carob chips

1oz/25g wheatgerm

1 tablespoon maple syrup

1 tablespoon soya milk

1 dessertspoon coffee powder

Cream the margarine with the sugar and maple syrup. Add the sifted flour and coffee powder, the wheatgerm, carob chips and soya milk and mix thoroughly until all ingredients bind together.

Divide the mixture into 12 equal portions and roll each one into a ball in the palm of the hand. Flatten the balls to form biscuits and put them on a greased baking sheet. Bake in a preheated oven at 180°C/350°F/Gas mark 4 for 10–12 minutes until browned. Transfer to a wire rack.

Sesame seed and oat crunchies

Makes approx 16

2oz/50g sesame seeds

2oz/50g porridge oats

2oz/50g medium oatmeal

2oz/50g oatbran

2oz/50g fine wholemeal self raising flour

2oz/50g vegan margarine

1oz/25g demerara sugar

1 rounded tablespoon golden syrup

3 tablespoons soya milk

Melt the margarine, sugar and golden syrup in a large saucepan. Remove from the heat and stir in the dry ingredients, then add the soya milk. Mix thoroughly until the mixture binds together. Shape rounded dessertspoonfuls of the mixture into flat rounds. Place these on a greased baking sheet and bake in a preheated oven at 180°C/350°F/Gas mark 4 for 10–12 minutes until golden. Carefully put on a wire rack to cool.

Sunflower and sesame snaps   *Makes approx 20*

4oz/100g fine wholemeal self raising flour

2oz/50g sunflower seeds, ground

2oz/50g vegan margarine

1oz/25g light muscovado sugar

1 rounded tablespoon tahini

2 tablespoons soya milk

extra soya milk

sesame seeds

Cream the margarine with the sugar and tahini, add the flour and ground sunflower seeds and then the 2 tablespoonfuls of soya milk. Mix well until a soft dough forms. Turn out onto a floured board and roll out to about ¼ inch/5mm thick. Cut into circles with a 2¼ inch/5.5cm biscuit cutter and keep gathering up the remaining dough and re-rolling it until it is used up. Put the circles on a greased baking sheet and brush them with soya milk. Sprinkle with sesame seeds and bake in a preheated oven at 180°C/350°F/Gas mark 4 for 12–15 minutes until golden. Leave to cool on a wire rack.

TRAY BAKES

Chewy muesli fingers

Makes 10

- 2oz/50g wheat flakes
- 2oz/50g barley flakes
- 2oz/50g oatbran
- 2oz/50g sultanas, chopped
- 1oz/25g dried dates, finely chopped
- 1oz/25g sunflower seeds
- 1oz/25g sesame seeds
- 1oz/25g mixed nuts, finely chopped
- 1oz/25g wheatgerm
- 1oz/25g soya flour
- 4 tablespoons sunflower oil
- 2 rounded tablespoons golden syrup
- 1 rounded tablespoon malt extract
- 5 fl.oz/150ml soya milk
- 1 teaspoon vanilla essence

Gently heat the sunflower oil, golden syrup, malt extract and vanilla essence in a large saucepan and stir until well combined. Remove from the heat, add the remaining ingredients and mix thoroughly. Spoon the mixture into a lined and greased 7 inch/18cm square flan tin, pressing down firmly and evenly with the back of the spoon. Bake in a preheated oven at 170°C/325°F/Gas mark 3 for about 20 minutes until golden. Turn out onto a wire rack and cut into 10 equal-sized fingers when cold.

Apple and date parkin

Makes 10

8oz/225g eating apples, peeled, cored and grated

6oz/175g medium oatmeal

4oz/100g fine wholemeal self raising flour

3oz/75g vegan margarine

2oz/50g dried dates, finely chopped

1oz/25g demerara sugar

2 rounded tablespoons molasses

2 rounded tablespoons golden syrup

1 tablespoon fresh apple juice

1 rounded teaspoon ground ginger

Put the margarine, sugar, molasses and golden syrup in a large saucepan and heat gently until melted. Remove from the heat and add the sifted flour and ground ginger and then the remaining ingredients. Mix thoroughly, then spoon the mixture into a lined and greased 7 inch/18cm square flan tin. Press down firmly and evenly and bake in a preheated oven at 180°C/350°F/Gas mark 4 for approximately 25 minutes until firm in the centre. Turn out onto a wire rack and allow to cool. Cut into 10 equal-sized slices.

Malted fruit and coconut slices

Makes 8

8oz/225g mixed cake fruit

4oz/100g fine wholemeal self raising flour

2oz/50g vegan margarine

1oz/25g demerara sugar

1oz/25g desiccated coconut

1/2oz/15g soya flour

3 tablespoons water

3 tablespoons fresh fruit juice

1 rounded tablespoon malt extract

extra desiccated coconut

Put the malt extract, margarine and sugar in a saucepan. Heat gently until melted and remove from the heat. Whisk the soya flour with the water until smooth and add to the saucepan together with the mixed fruit, flour, 1oz/25g coconut and fruit juice. Mix thoroughly, then spoon the mixture evenly into a lined and greased 7 inch/18cm square flan tin. Sprinkle the top lightly with desiccated coconut and press this in slightly with the back of a spoon. Bake in a preheated oven at 170°C/325°F/Gas mark 3 for about 25 minutes until browned. Cool on a wire rack and cut into 8 equal-sized slices to serve.

Courgette, orange and date slice   *Makes 8*

base
2oz/50g medium oatmeal
2oz/50g porridge oats
1oz/25g vegan margarine
2 tablespoons soya milk

filling
4oz/100g dried dates
juice of 1 large orange

topping
4oz/100g courgette, grated
4oz/100g fine wholemeal self raising flour
1oz/25g vegan margarine
1oz/25g light muscovado sugar
$^1/_2$oz/15g soya flour
3 tablespoons fresh orange juice
finely grated peel of 1 orange
2 tablespoons soya milk
$^1/_4$ teaspoon grated nutmeg
sesame seeds

Melt the margarine over a low heat, then stir in the oatmeal and porridge oats, add the milk and mix thoroughly. Spoon the mixture into a lined and greased

7 inch/18cm square flan tin. Spread it out evenly and press down firmly with the back of a spoon.

Put the dates and orange juice in a small saucepan and bring to the boil. Cover and simmer gently for about 10 minutes until the juice has been absorbed and the dates are soft. Mash them with the back of a spoon and spread them evenly over the base mixture in the tin.

Cream the margarine with the sugar. Whisk the soya flour with the orange juice until thick and creamy, add to the bowl and mix thoroughly. Stir in the courgette and orange peel, then the sifted flour and nutmeg. Finally, add the soya milk and mix everything very well. Spoon the topping evenly over the dates, covering them completely. Sprinkle sesame seeds on top, then bake in a preheated oven at 180°C/350°F/Gas mark 4 for about 35 minutes until golden brown. Turn out onto a wire rack and cut into 8 equal slices when cold.

Mincemeat and maple squares   *Makes 9*

base

3oz/75g fine wholemeal self raising flour

1oz/25g vegan margarine

soya milk

filling

8oz/225g mincemeat

topping

4oz/100g fine wholemeal self raising flour

2oz/50g vegan margarine

1oz/25g medium oatmeal

1oz/25g porridge oats

3 tablespoons maple syrup

4 fl.oz/125ml soya milk

Make the base by rubbing the margarine into the flour and adding enough soya milk to bind. Turn out onto a floured board and roll out to fit a lined and greased 7 inch/18cm square flan tin. Spread evenly with the mincemeat.

Gently melt the maple syrup and margarine in a large saucepan. Remove from the heat and add the remaining topping ingredients. Mix thoroughly, then spread the mixture over the mincemeat. Bake in a preheated oven at 180°C/350°F/Gas mark 4 for about 30 minutes until golden. Leave on a wire rack to cool, then cut into 9 squares.

Ginger and date bars   *Makes 8*

> 6oz/175g fine wholemeal self raising flour
> 4oz/100g dried dates, finely chopped
> 2oz/50g vegan margarine
> 2oz/50g stem ginger, finely chopped
> 1oz/25g stem ginger, finely sliced
> 1oz/25g demerara sugar
> 4 fl.oz/125ml water
> 3 fl.oz/75ml soya milk

Put the dates and water in a small saucepan, bring to the boil and simmer for a couple of minutes whilst stirring until the dates become pulpy and the mixture thickens. Mash the dates with the back of a spoon until smooth.

Melt the margarine and sugar in another saucepan, then remove from the heat, add the date purée, chopped ginger, flour and soya milk and mix thoroughly. Spoon the dough evenly into a lined and greased 7 inch/18cm square flan tin. Level the mixture and arrange the ginger slices on top, pressing them in lightly. Bake in a preheated oven at 170°C/325°F/Gas mark 3 for about 30 minutes until golden brown and firm in the centre. Turn out onto a wire rack and cut into 8 equal-sized bars when cold.

cot and marzipan oat squares *Makes 9*

4oz/100g dried apricots

4oz/100g porridge oats

4oz/100g fine wholemeal self raising flour

2oz/50g marzipan, chilled and grated

2oz/50g vegan margarine

1/2oz/15g soya flour

1 rounded tablespoon golden syrup

6 tablespoons fresh orange juice

Soak the apricots in water for 15 minutes, drain and chop very finely. Put the margarine and golden syrup in a large saucepan and heat gently until melted. Remove from the heat and stir in the porridge oats, self raising flour, marzipan and apricots. Mix the soya flour with the orange juice and add. Combine well, then spoon the mixture into a lined and greased 7 inch/18cm square flan tin. Press down firmly and evenly and bake in a preheated oven at 180°C/350°F/Gas mark 4 for 18–20 minutes until golden. Turn out onto a wire rack and allow to cool. Carefully cut into 9 equal squares.

Carob and apple brownies *Makes 9*

8oz/225g fine wholemeal self raising flour

8oz/225g cooking apple, peeled, cored and grated

4oz/100g vegan margarine

3oz/75g demerara sugar

2oz/50g sultanas, chopped

1/2oz/15g soya flour

4 tablespoons fresh apple juice

1 rounded tablespoon carob powder

11/2oz/40g carob bar, broken

Sift the flour and carob powder into a mixing bowl, rub in the margarine and stir in the sugar, apple and sultanas. Whisk the soya flour with the apple juice until smooth, then add to the other ingredients and mix thoroughly. Spoon the mixture into a lined and greased 7 inch/18cm square flan tin and level the top. Bake in a preheated oven at 180°C/350°F/Gas mark 4 for 30 minutes. Put on a wire rack until cold.

Melt the carob bar in a bowl over a pan of boiling water. Spread the melted carob evenly over the top of the cake and keep in the fridge for about an hour until the carob has set. Cut into 9 squares to serve.

Crumbly apricot slices   *Makes 8*

4oz/100g fine wholemeal self raising flour

4oz/100g wholewheat semolina

3oz/75g vegan margarine

1oz/25g demerara sugar

1 rounded tablespoon golden syrup

1 tablespoon soya milk

$1/2$ teaspoon ground cinnamon

filling

4oz/100g dried apricots, finely chopped

6 fl.oz/175ml fresh orange juice

Put the apricots and orange juice in a saucepan and leave for 30 minutes. Then bring to the boil, cover and simmer gently for 10–15 minutes until the juice has been absorbed and the apricots are soft. Mash them with the back of a spoon and set aside.

Gently heat the margarine and golden syrup in a large saucepan until melted. Remove from the heat and add the semolina, sugar, sifted flour and cinnamon. Mix thoroughly, then sprinkle on the milk and stir lightly. Spoon just over half of the mixture into a lined and greased 7 inch/18cm square flan tin and press down firmly and evenly with the back of a spoon. Spread the apricot mixture over this base. Crumble the remaining mixture over the top and press down lightly. Bake in a preheated oven at 180°C/350°F/Gas mark 4 for about 20 minutes until golden. Allow to cool in the tin, then transfer to a wire rack to get completely cold. Cut into 8 equal-sized slices.

Parsnip and banana slice

Serves 8

6oz/175g parsnip, peeled and grated

4oz/100g fine wholemeal self raising flour

2oz/50g soya flakes

2oz/50g vegan margarine

1¹/₂oz/40g light muscovado sugar

1oz/25g desiccated coconut

¹/₂oz/15g soya flour

4 fl.oz/125ml soya milk

3 tablespoons fresh apple juice

filling

4oz/100g dried bananas, finely chopped

5 fl.oz./150ml fresh apple juice

Put the dried bananas and apple juice in a small saucepan, bring to the boil, cover and simmer for about 15 minutes until the juice has been absorbed and the bananas are soft. Remove from the heat and mash.

Bring the parsnip and soya milk to the boil in another saucepan. Cover and simmer for 3 minutes. Remove from the heat and allow to cool.

Cream the margarine with the sugar and stir in the parsnip, flour, soya flakes and coconut. Whisk the soya flour with the apple juice and add, mixing thoroughly. Spoon half the mixture evenly into a lined and greased 7 inch/18cm square flan tin, then the banana, and finish with the other half of the mixture, spreading it out evenly. Bake in a preheated oven at 180°C/350°F/Gas mark 4 for about 35 minutes until golden brown. Turn out onto a wire rack to cool. Cut into 8 slices to serve.

Malted date and almond bars   *Makes 8*

4oz/100g fine wholemeal self raising flour

4oz/100g dried dates, finely chopped

2oz/50g ground almonds

2oz/50g vegan margarine

1oz/25g demerara sugar

1oz/25g soya flour

1 rounded tablespoon malt extract

5 fl.oz/150ml soya milk

$^{1}/_{2}$oz/15g flaked almonds

Melt the malt extract, margarine and sugar in a large saucepan over a gentle heat. Take off the stove and add the remaining ingredients except the flaked almonds. Mix thoroughly, then spoon the mixture into a lined and greased 7 inch/18cm square flan tin. Level the top, sprinkle with the flaked almonds and press these in lightly. Bake in a preheated oven at 170°C/325°F/Gas mark 3 for about 25 minutes until browned. Allow to cool on a wire rack, then cut into 8 equal sized-bars.

Cashew nut and banana squares

Makes 9

1 banana (approx. 8oz/225g), peeled and mashed

4oz/100g fine wholemeal self raising flour

2oz/50g cashew nuts, grated

2oz/50g vegan margarine

1oz/25g light muscovado sugar

1oz/25g soya flour

4 fl.oz/125ml soya milk

$^1/_2$oz/15g cashew nuts, halved

Put the margarine and sugar in a large saucepan and heat gently until melted. Remove from the heat and stir in the mashed banana and grated cashews. Mix the soya flour with the soya milk until smooth and add, together with the flour. Stir thoroughly, then spoon the mixture evenly into a lined and greased 7 inch/18cm square flan tin. Sprinkle the cashew nut halves on top and press these in lightly with the back of a spoon. Bake in a preheated oven at 180°C/350°F/Gas mark 4 for about 25 minutes until golden. Carefully transfer to a wire rack and cut into 9 squares when cold.

Nutty apple and sultana slices

Makes 8

8oz/225g cooking apple, peeled, cored and grated

4oz/100g fine wholemeal self raising flour

2oz/50g mixed nuts, grated

2oz/50g sultanas

1oz/25g light muscovado sugar

1oz/25g soya flour

4 tablespoons sunflower oil

1 rounded tablespoon golden syrup

2 fl.oz/50ml fresh apple juice

$^1/_2$ teaspoon ground cinnamon

Gently heat the oil, sugar and golden syrup in a large saucepan whilst stirring to combine. Remove from the heat and stir in the apple and sultanas and three-quarters of the grated nuts. Whisk the soya flour with the apple juice and add to the pan together with the sifted flour and cinnamon. Mix thoroughly, then spoon the mixture evenly into a lined and greased 7 inch/18cm square flan tin. Sprinkle the remaining grated nuts on top and press them in lightly with the back of a spoon. Bake in a preheated oven at 170°C/325°F/Gas mark 3 for about 30 minutes until golden brown. Leave on a wire rack to cool, then cut into 8 equal slices.

Fig and coconut oat slices   *Makes 8*

6oz/175g porridge oats

2oz/50g desiccated coconut

2oz/50g vegan margarine

1oz/25g muscovado sugar

2 rounded tablespoons golden syrup

3 tablespoons soya milk

filling

6oz/175g dried figs, finely chopped

5 fl.oz/150ml fresh orange juice

Put the figs and orange juice in a saucepan and bring to the boil, cover and simmer gently until the figs are pulpy and the juice has been absorbed. Remove from the heat and mash.

Heat the margarine, sugar and golden syrup in a large saucepan until melted. Remove from the heat and stir in the porridge oats and coconut, add the milk and mix thoroughly. Spoon just over half of the mixture into a lined and greased 7 inch/18cm square flan tin, pressing down firmly and evenly with the back of the spoon. Spread the mashed figs over this base, then spoon over the rest of the mixture and press down firmly. Bake in a preheated oven at 180°C/350°F/Gas mark 4 for about 25 minutes until golden. Leave to cool in the tin, then transfer to a wire rack to get completely cold. Cut into 8 equal-sized slices to serve.

Dried banana and walnut bars   *Makes 8*

> 6oz/175g fine wholemeal self raising flour
> 4oz/100g dried bananas, finely chopped
> 2oz/50g vegan margarine
> 1oz/25g light muscovado sugar
> 1oz/25g walnuts, finely chopped
> ¹/₂oz/15g soya flour
> 9 fl.oz/250ml strong black tea
> 4 fl.oz/125ml soya milk

Put the dried bananas and tea in a saucepan, bring to the boil and simmer gently until the liquid has been almost absorbed and the bananas are pulpy. Remove from the heat and mash.

Cream the margarine with the sugar. Add the mashed bananas and walnuts and stir well. Whisk the soya flour with the milk and add together with the flour. Mix thoroughly and spoon the mixture evenly into a lined and greased 7 inch/18cm square flan tin. Bake in a preheated oven at 180°C/350°F/Gas mark 4 for about 30 minutes until firm in the centre. Cool on a wire rack and cut into 8 bars.

Apple and ginger bread pudding   *Serves 8*

8oz/225g eating apple, peeled, cored and grated

8oz/225g fresh wholemeal breadcrumbs

8oz/225g mixed cake fruit

2oz/50g stem ginger, finely chopped

2oz/50g vegan margarine

1oz/25g demerara sugar

$^1/_2$oz/15g soya flour

3 tablespoons water

2 tablespoons fresh apple juice

1 rounded tablespoon golden syrup

1 rounded teaspoon ground mixed spice

1 rounded teaspoon ground cinnamon

extra demerara sugar (optional)

Cream the margarine with the sugar and golden syrup. Combine the soya flour with the water until smooth and add, together with the apple, bread-crumbs, mixed cake fruit, ginger, apple juice and spices. Mix very well, then spoon the mixture into a lined and greased 9 x 6 inch/23 x 15cm baking tin. Press down firmly and evenly and sprinkle the top with a little demerara sugar if desired. Bake in a preheated oven at 180°C/350°F/Gas mark 4 for about 40 minutes until golden brown. Leave in the tin to cool slightly, then put on a wire rack until cold. Cut into 8 equal portions.

Banana bread pudding

Omit the apple, ginger and apple juice from the recipe for apple and ginger bread pudding and add 8oz/225g banana, peeled and mashed.

Mincemeat bread pudding

Omit the apple, mixed cake fruit, ginger and sugar from the apple and ginger bread pudding recipe and add 1lb/450g mincemeat.

Sultana flapjacks   *Makes 8*

6oz/175g porridge oats

2oz/50g vegan margarine

2oz/50g sultanas, chopped

1oz/25g demerara sugar

2 rounded tablespoons golden syrup

Heat the margarine, sugar and golden syrup gently in a saucepan until melted. Remove from the heat and stir in the porridge oats and sultanas. Mix thoroughly and spoon the mixture into a lined and greased 7 inch/18cm square flan tin. Press down firmly and evenly with the back of a spoon. Bake in a preheated oven at 180°C/350°F/Gas mark 4 for about 15 minutes until golden. Leave in the tin for 15 minutes, then cut into 8 equal-sized bars and put them on a wire rack to cool completely.

Apple, ginger and sultana flapjacks

Ingredients as for sultana flapjacks, plus

8oz/225g cooking apple, peeled, cored and grated

1/2oz/15g stem ginger, finely chopped

Follow the instructions in the previous recipe but bake for 30–35 rather than 15 minutes.

NO-BAKE CAKES

Almond truffle cake   *Serves 8*

9oz/250g marzipan

8oz/225g vegan fruit cake, crumbled

8oz/225g vegan mincemeat

4oz/100g ground almonds

3oz/75g flaked brown rice

2 tablespoons fresh fruit juice

2oz/50g carob bar, broken

1/2oz/15g toasted flaked almonds

Put the cake crumbs, mincemeat, ground almonds, flaked brown rice and fruit juice in a mixing bowl and combine well.

Take three-quarters of the marzipan and roll out to line a 7 inch/18cm diameter loose-bottomed flan tin that has been lined with cling film. Spoon the cake mixture into the marzipan 'case' and press down firmly and evenly. Fold any overhanging marzipan towards the centre to enclose the filling and roll out the remaining piece of marzipan into a circle to cover, pinching to join. Carefully invert the cake onto a plate and remove the cling film.

Melt the carob bar in a bowl over a pan of boiling water and spread it evenly over the top and sides of the cake. Sprinkle the flaked almonds on top and put in the fridge for a few hours or overnight until set.

Banana and brazil nut bites

Makes 12

4oz/100g dried banana, finely chopped

7 fl.oz/200ml fresh apple juice

4oz/100g soya flakes, ground

2oz/50g brazil nuts, grated

2oz/50g fine oatmeal

Put the banana and apple juice in a small saucepan and bring to the boil. Cover and simmer gently for approximately 15 minutes until the juice has been absorbed and the bananas are soft. Remove from the heat and mash with a potato masher. Transfer to a mixing bowl and work in the soya flakes, brazil nuts and oatmeal. Mix thoroughly until the mixture is well combined and stiff. Take heaped dessertspoonfuls and roll into balls in the palm of the hand. Put the balls on a plate, cover with cling film and refrigerate for a few hours. Serve in paper cake cases.

Sherry and nut truffles

Makes 12

1lb/450g vegan fruit cake

4oz/100g sugar-free jam

2oz/50g mixed nuts, grated

1oz/25g cocoa powder

4 tablespoons sherry

finely grated nuts or carob bar

Mix the jam and sherry well. Crumble the cake into fine crumbs and add to the bowl together with the 2oz/50g grated nuts and the sifted cocoa powder. Mix thoroughly until everything binds together. Take heaped tablespoonfuls of the mixture and roll into balls in the palm of the hand. Roll each ball in finely grated nuts or carob bar until completely covered. Put on a plate, cover and chill for a couple of hours or overnight until firm. Transfer to paper cake cases to serve.

Peach and walnut oat rounds   *Makes 10*

4oz/100g porridge oats

2oz/50g medium oatmeal

2oz/50g dried peaches, finely chopped

1oz/50g walnuts, grated

1oz/25g vegan margarine

1 tablespoon golden syrup

8 fl.oz/225ml fresh orange juice

Leave the peaches to soak in the orange juice in a small saucepan for 30 minutes, then bring to the boil, cover and simmer for about 20 minutes until the juice has been absorbed and the peaches are soft, stirring frequently to prevent sticking. Remove from the heat and mash until smooth.

Put the margarine and golden syrup into another saucepan and heat gently until melted. Remove from the heat and stir in the mashed peaches, add the porridge oats, oatmeal and walnuts and mix thoroughly. Spoon a heaped dessertspoonful of the mixture into a 2¹/₄ inch/5.5cm diameter biscuit cutter which has been placed on a plate. Press the mixture down firmly until it fills the round shape. Turn the cutter over and press the other side down firmly. Remove the round and neaten if necessary, then put it on a tray. Repeat with the remaining mixture. Cover the rounds with cling film and leave in the fridge for a few hours until set.

Date and peanut oatmeal fingers   *Makes 12*

1lb/450g medium oatmeal

4oz/100g dried dates, finely chopped

4oz/100g roasted shelled peanuts, toasted and ground

2oz/50g vegan margarine

5 fl.oz/150ml fresh apple juice

1 rounded tablespoon peanut butter

1 tablespoon date syrup

Bring the dates and apple juice to the boil in a small saucepan and simmer for about 5 minutes whilst stirring until the mixture thickens. Remove from the heat and mash the dates with the back of a spoon.

Put the margarine, peanut butter and date syrup in a large saucepan and heat gently until melted. Remove from the heat and stir in the date mixture and the ground peanuts. Gradually add the oatmeal until a very stiff mixture is obtained. Spoon this into a lined 7 inch/18cm square flan tin and press it down firmly and evenly. Cover and refrigerate overnight. Cut the square into 12 equal-sized fingers to serve.

Pineapple and coconut wedges   *Makes 6*

> 4oz/100g dried pineapple, finely chopped
> 6 fl.oz/175ml fresh pineapple juice
> 2oz/50g desiccated coconut
> 2oz/50g porridge oats
> 1oz/25g vegan margarine

Put the chopped pineapple and pineapple juice in a saucepan and bring to the boil. Cover and simmer for about 20–25 minutes, stirring frequently to prevent sticking, until the juice has been absorbed and the pineapple is soft. Remove from the heat and mash. Add the margarine and stir until melted, then stir in the coconut and porridge oats and mix thoroughly. Spoon the mixture into a lined 7 inch/18cm diameter flan tin. Press down firmly and evenly, cover and keep in the fridge for a few hours or overnight. Cut into 6 equal wedges.

Sultana and bran flapjack   *Serves 6*

4oz/100g sultanas, finely chopped
4oz/100g porridge oats
2oz/50g bran sticks
2 fl.oz/50ml fresh fruit juice
1oz/25g vegan margarine
1 rounded tablespoon golden syrup

Soak the bran sticks in the fruit juice for 10 minutes. Stir frequently so that all the sticks soften.

Heat the margarine and golden syrup in a large saucepan until melted. Remove from the heat and add the bran sticks, porridge oats and sultanas. Mix well, then spoon the mixture into a lined 7 inch/18cm diameter flan tin. Press down firmly and evenly, cover and put in the fridge for a couple of hours or overnight. Cut into 6 wedges to serve.

Apricot and almond oat squares   *Makes 9*

6oz/175g porridge oats
4oz/100g dried apricots, finely chopped
4oz/100g ground almonds
2oz/50g vegan margarine
6 fl.oz/175ml fresh orange juice
1 rounded tablespoon golden syrup

Put the dried apricots and fruit juice in a saucepan and bring to the boil. Cover and simmer gently until the juice has been absorbed and the apricots are soft. Stir frequently to prevent sticking. Remove from the heat and mash the apricots.

Gently heat the margarine and golden syrup in a large saucepan until melted. Remove from the heat and stir in the mashed apricots, add the porridge oats and ground almonds and mix thoroughly until a very stiff mixture is formed. Spoon this into a lined 7 inch/18cm square flan tin, pressing down firmly and evenly. Cover and refrigerate overnight, then cut into 9 squares.

Tropical fruit and nut balls   *Makes 8*

4oz/100g dried mango, finely chopped

7 fl.oz/200ml tropical fruit juice

2oz/50g brazil nuts, grated

2oz/50g fine oatmeal

2oz/50g porridge oats

1oz/25g desiccated coconut

toasted desiccated coconut

Bring the mango to the boil in the fruit juice, cover and simmer gently whilst stirring frequently for up to 30 minutes until the juice has been absorbed and the mango is soft. Remove from the heat and mash with a potato masher. Add the brazil nuts, oatmeal, porridge oats and 1oz/25g coconut and mix thoroughly until well combined and stiff. Take heaped dessertspoonfuls of the mixture and roll into balls in the palm of the hand, then roll each ball in the toasted coconut until completely covered. Chill for a couple of hours to firm. Serve in paper cake cases.

Date and mocha biscuit wedges   *Makes 8*

4oz/100g plain vegan biscuits, crushed

2oz/50g dried dates, finely chopped

2oz/50g vegan margarine

1oz/25g vegan chocolate bar, broken

1 tablespoon date syrup

1 tablespoon cocoa powder

1 rounded teaspoon coffee powder

Gently heat the margarine, chocolate bar, date syrup, cocoa powder and coffee powder in a saucepan until melted and well combined. Remove from the heat and stir in the biscuits and dates. Mix thoroughly, then spoon the mixture into a lined 7 inch/18cm diameter flan tin, pressing it down firmly and evenly with the back of the spoon. Cover and leave in the fridge overnight until set. Cut into 8 wedges to serve.

Pear and apple squares   *Makes 9*

> 6oz/175g wheat flakes, crushed
>
> 4oz/100g dried pears, finely chopped
>
> 2oz/50g dried apple, finely chopped
>
> 2oz/50g pear and apple spread
>
> 1oz/25g vegan margarine
>
> 5 fl.oz/150ml fresh apple juice

Put the dried pear and apple juice in a saucepan and bring to the boil. Stir well, cover and simmer gently for about 15 minutes until the juice has been absorbed and the pears are soft. Remove from the heat and mash until smooth.

Heat the pear and apple spread and the margarine in a large saucepan whilst stirring, until well combined. Remove from the heat and stir in the pear mixture, then the dried apple and crushed wheat flakes and mix well until stiff. Spoon the mixture into a lined 7 inch/18cm square flan tin and press it down firmly and evenly. Cover and keep in the fridge for a few hours or overnight to set. Cut into 9 equal squares.

Carob crispies   *Makes 8*

> 1¹/₂oz/40g carob bar, broken
>
> 1¹/₂oz/40g rice crispies
>
> 1oz/25g vegan margarine
>
> 1 rounded tablespoon golden syrup

Put the carob bar, margarine and golden syrup in a large saucepan and heat gently until melted. Remove from the heat and stir in the rice crispies, then spoon the mixture into 8 paper cake cases that have been put into muffin tins. Cover with cling film and chill for a few hours until set.

Chocolate, peanut and sultana bars   *Makes 10*

6oz/175g shelled peanuts, ground

4oz/100g medium oatmeal

3oz/75g vegan chocolate bar, broken

2oz/50g porridge oats

2oz/50g sultanas, finely chopped

2oz/50g vegan margarine

2 rounded tablespoons peanut butter

Gently heat the chocolate bar, margarine and peanut butter in a large saucepan until melted. Remove from the heat and add the remaining ingredients. Mix well and spread the mixture into a lined 7 inch/18cm square flan tin. Press down firmly and evenly with the back of a spoon. Cover with cling film and refrigerate for a few hours. Cut into 10 equal-sized bars with a sharp knife.

Wholewheat coconut and carob bars   *Makes 10*

6 wholewheat breakfast biscuits, crushed

3oz/75g carob bar, broken

3oz/75g vegan margarine

2oz/50g desiccated coconut

2 rounded tablespoons carob spread

Melt the carob bar, margarine and carob spread in a large saucepan. Remove from the heat and add the breakfast biscuits and coconut. Mix thoroughly, then put the mixture into a lined 7 inch/18cm square flan tin, pressing it down firmly and evenly with the back of a spoon. Cover with cling film and leave in the fridge for a few hours until set, then cut into 10 bars with a sharp knife.

SAVOURY BAKING

Olive and oregano bread

1 1/2lb/675g plain unbleached white flour

1 sachet easy-blend yeast

4 tablespoons olive oil

1 teaspoon salt

10 black olives

10 green olives

1 dessertspoon oregano

approx. 12 fl.oz/350ml warm water

extra olive oil

Mix the flour, yeast, salt and oregano in a large bowl. Keep 4 olives and finely chop the rest. Add the chopped olives and 4 tablespoonfuls of olive oil to the dry ingredients and mix well, then gradually add the water until a soft dough forms. Turn this out onto a floured board and knead. Return it to the bowl and cover with a piece of oiled cling film. Leave in a warm place for 1 hour until risen. Again turn the dough out onto a floured board and knead, then shape it into a circle of about 10 inches/25cm in diameter. Transfer to an oiled baking sheet, cover with oiled cling film and leave in a warm place for 30 minutes. Cut the remaining olives in half and press these into the top of the dough. Brush with olive oil and bake in a preheated oven at 200°C/400°F/Gas mark 6 for approximately 25 minutes until golden brown. Transfer to a wire rack and allow to cool before slicing.

Savoury sesame sticks   *Makes 16*

> 4oz/100g fine wholemeal self raising flour
>
> 1oz/25g vegan margarine
>
> 1oz/25g sesame seeds
>
> 1oz/25g vegan 'cheddar', grated
>
> 1/2 teaspoon paprika
>
> 1/2 teaspoon soy sauce
>
> 3 tablespoons water

Rub the margarine into the flour. Stir in the sesame seeds, grated 'cheddar' and paprika, add the soy sauce and water and mix until a soft dough forms. Turn out onto a floured board and roll out to a square measuring 9 x 8 inches/23 x 20cm. Cut the dough into 16 sticks of 4¹/₂ x 1 inch/11.5 x 2.5cm. Transfer the sticks to a greased baking sheet and squeeze the long edges of each stick towards the centre to give the edges a wavy effect. Bake in a preheated oven at 180°C/350°F/Gas mark 4 for about 15 minutes until golden. Carefully put onto a wire rack and allow to cool.

Onion, sage and walnut scones   *Makes 12*

> 8oz/225g fine wholemeal self raising flour
>
> 2oz/50g vegan margarine
>
> 1oz/25g walnuts, finely chopped
>
> 1 dessertspoon dried sage
>
> 1 onion, peeled and grated
>
> 1 dessertspoon olive oil
>
> approx. 6 tablespoons soya milk
>
> extra soya milk

Heat the oil and gently fry the onion until softened. Rub the margarine into the flour, stir in the sage, walnuts and onion and gradually add the milk until a soft dough forms. Turn out onto a floured board and roll out to approximately ³/₄ inch/2cm thick. Cut into 2 inch/5cm rounds with a biscuit cutter. Put the rounds on a greased baking sheet, gather up the remaining dough and re-roll until it is all used up. Brush the top of the scones with soya milk and bake in a preheated oven at 180°C/350°F/Gas mark 4 for about 15 minutes until golden brown. Leave to cool on a wire rack.

Almond oatcakes

Makes approx 22

4oz/100g medium oatmeal

2oz/50g porridge oats

2oz/50g fine wholemeal self raising flour

2oz/50g vegan margarine

1 rounded tablespoon almond butter

1/2 teaspoon yeast extract

3 tablespoons water

Gently heat the margarine, nut butter and yeast extract in a saucepan until melted. Remove from the heat and stir in the oatmeal, oats and flour, then add the water and mix until it binds together. Turn out onto a floured board and roll out to about 1/4 inch/5mm thick. Cut into 2 inch/5cm rounds with a biscuit cutter and transfer the rounds to a greased baking sheet. Gather up and re-roll the dough until used up. Bake in a preheated oven at 180°C/350°F/Gas mark 4 for 10–12 minutes until golden. Leave for 5 minutes, then carefully put on a wire rack and allow to cool completely.

Pepper and pesto buns

Makes 12

8oz/225g plain wholemeal flour

4oz/100g mixed peppers, finely chopped

2oz/50g vegan margarine, melted

1 rounded teaspoon easy-blend yeast

1 rounded dessertspoon vegan pesto

1 dessertspoon olive oil

1/4 teaspoon salt

10 fl.oz/300ml soya milk, warmed

sesame seeds

Heat the olive oil in a pan and gently fry the peppers until soft. Add the pesto and stir until well combined. Mix the flour, yeast and salt in a large bowl and add the pepper and pesto mixture, melted margarine and warmed soya milk. Stir thoroughly until a thick batter forms. Divide this between the 12 holes of a greased muffin tin and sprinkle with sesame seeds. Leave in a warm place for 1 hour until risen, then bake in a preheated oven at 180°C/350°F/Gas mark 4 for about 25 minutes until golden brown. Run a sharp knife around the edges and turn the buns out onto a wire rack.

Herby garlic and Parmesan breadsticks   *Makes 36*

1lb/450g plain unbleached white flour

2 teaspoons easy-blend yeast

1/2 teaspoon salt

2 rounded teaspoons dried mixed herbs

2 tablespoons vegan 'Parmesan'

3 tablespoons olive oil

2 garlic cloves, crushed

approx. 10 fl.oz/300ml warm water

Put the flour, yeast, salt, herbs, 'Parmesan' and garlic in a large bowl and mix. Stir in the oil, then gradually add the water until a soft dough forms. Turn out onto a floured board and knead well. Return to the bowl, cover with a piece of oiled cling film and leave in a warm place for 1 hour until risen. Turn out onto a floured board and knead again. Divide the dough into 36 equal pieces and roll each piece into a stick of about 8 inches/20cm. Put the sticks on an oiled baking sheet and leave in a warm place for 30 minutes. Bake in a preheated oven at 200°C/400°F/Gas mark 6 for approximately 20 minutes until golden and crisp. Serve warm or cold.

Courgette and caraway muffins

Makes 8

6oz/175g fine wholemeal self raising flour

4oz/100g courgette, grated

2oz/50g vegan margarine, melted

^{1}/$_2$oz/15g soya flour

3 tablespoons water

4 fl.oz/125ml soya milk

1 rounded teaspoon caraway seeds

1 dessertspoon soy sauce

sesame seeds

Put the flour, courgette and caraway seeds in a mixing bowl and stir in the melted margarine. Mix the soya flour with the water and soy sauce and add to the bowl, together with the soya milk. Stir well, then divide the mixture between 8 holes of a greased muffin tin. Sprinkle sesame seeds on top of the muffins and bake in a preheated oven at 180°C/350°F/Gas mark 4 for about 25 minutes until golden brown. Carefully transfer to a wire rack to cool.

Sun-dried tomato and herb rolls

Makes 12

1lb/450g plain unbleached white flour

8oz/225g plain wholemeal flour

2oz/50g sun-dried tomatoes, finely chopped

1 sachet easy-blend yeast

4 tablespoons olive oil

1 dessertspoon sun-dried tomato paste

1 dessertspoon herbes du Provence

1 teaspoon salt

approx. 15 fl.oz/450ml warm water

extra olive oil

Soak the tomatoes in the 4 tablespoonfuls olive oil for 2 hours. Put the flours, yeast, herbs and salt into a mixing bowl and stir. Add the soaked tomatoes and

remaining oil and mix in. Dissolve the tomato paste in the water and gradually add to the mixture until a soft dough forms. Turn this out onto a floured
board and knead well. Return it to the bowl, cover with a piece of oiled cling
film and leave in a warm place for 1 hour until risen.

Knead the dough again, then divide it into 12 equal pieces. Roll each piece into
a round in the palm of the hand. Arrange 9 of the rounds in a circle on a
greased baking sheet and place the remaining 3 in the centre. Squeeze the
whole shape together so that no gaps remain. Cover with oiled cling film and
leave in a warm place for an hour to rise. Brush the top with olive oil and bake
in a preheated oven at 200°C/400°F/Gas mark 6 for about 20 minutes until
golden and hollow sounding when tapped underneath. Put on a wire rack to
cool. Cut into the 12 separate rolls to serve.